LOVE THE UNFINISHED CHAPTER

"What Should've Been Told"

DR. LARON MATTHEWS, PHD

Love the Unfinished Chapter: What Should've Been Told

© December 2025

By Dr. Laron Matthews, PhD

Published in the United States of America

by LMM Publishing

ISBN: 978-1-945377-61-7

First Edition Printing

Printed in the United States of America

December 2025

Table of Contents

Special Dedication   1

Preface   2

Foreword by Bishop Zollie J. Keebler   3

Letters of Endorsement & Ministerial Support

Endorsement from Evangelist Dr. Gwen Marshall   7

Endorsement from Bishop Dr. Hurdis Bozeman   9

Endorsement from Dr. Samuel Hunter   10

Pastoral Reflection from Bishop Milton Lee Seaborne Sr.   12

Ministerial Endorsement from Dr. Marilyn Todman   14

Acknowledgments   16

Dedication   17

Chapter 1.   The Day the Blanket Fell Off the Bed   19

Chapter 2.   When Love Turned Into Luxury   25

Chapter 3.   The 911 Next to Me   31

Chapter 4.   When the Pillow Talk Ended   37

Chapter 5.   The Position I Once Loved, Now I Like It   43

Chapter 6.   Who Turned the Light Off in the Room   49

Chapter 7.   Who Turned the Light On in the Room   57

Chapter 8.   Who Stained the Sheets   63

Chapter 9.   When the Rings Got Lost   71

Chapter 10.   When the Seed Stopped Working and the
                Egg Started Wondering   79

Chapter 11.   The Day I Became Impotent   87

Chapter 12.   The Ceremony Is Over   95

Chapter 13.   Love — The Unfinished Chapter What
                Should've Been Told   103

Special Dedication

This book is lovingly dedicated to my father, Bishop Nathanel Matthews, and to the memory of my dear mother, Mother Suzanne Matthews. Their marriage of 64 years stands as a testament of covenant love, faith, and unwavering devotion. Dad, thank you for your steadfastness, strength, and faith. Mom, your presence is deeply missed, but your legacy continues to shine in our hearts and in the work of this ministry.

Preface

Love is both a gift and a calling. In these pages, you will not find a manual of theories, but a prophetic reflection on what it means to love with truth, passion, and covenantal depth. Each chapter represents a journey into the places where love has been tested, silenced, or forgotten, and offers a path to renewal and restoration.

My prayer is that this work will challenge, encourage, and awaken your heart to love in a way that reflects the very heart of God. May it lead you to rediscover covenant, rekindle intimacy, and embrace the unfinished chapters of love with faith and hope.

Foreword by Bishop Zollie J. Keebler

It is with great honor that I acknowledge the life, ministry, and testimony of my brother in Christ, Dr. Laron Matthews, PhD. In *Love: The Unfinished Chapter What Should've Have Been Told*, Dr. Matthews invites us into a sacred dialogue about love, covenant, and the challenges that test our faith and our marriages. His transparency is both courageous and needed in this generation.

As a bishop and shepherd of God's people, I see this work not merely as a book, but as a ministry — a tool for healing, restoration, and renewal. Those who read these pages will be reminded that love is not fragile when it is rooted in Christ, and that even unfinished chapters can become testimonies of God's grace.

I commend this work to every believer, every husband, every wife, and every leader who dares to embrace truth and transformation.

Bishop Zollie J. Keebler

House of Prayer, Prattville, Alabama

Letters of Endorsement
&
Ministerial Support

Endorsement from Evangelist Dr. Gwen Marshall

Love is not merely a gift we receive from God; it is the very nature of God Himself. To live in love is to live in Him. It must be generously lavished, freely given, and humbly embraced. The moment love is treated as a transaction, its essence is lost and the Holy Spirit quietly withdraws. This book is a call back to the divine rhythm of love.

In *Love: The Unfinished Chapter*, Prophet Dr. Laron Matthews writes not as a theorist, but as a prophetic witness. His words are both mirror and map: a mirror revealing where covenant has grown cold, and a map guiding us back to the altar of intimacy with God and with one another. Each chapter carries the pulse of heaven, reminding us that love is never static—it is always becoming, always maturing, always unfinished until Christ is revealed in us.

Communication is a sacred spice of love. When reduced to short waves, cautious remarks, or superficial exchanges, intimacy dies. But when speech flows from honesty, tenderness, and covenant faith, love thrives. This book restores that flow. It teaches us that the master bedroom is not a courtroom of performance, but a sanctuary of presence. It is the place where love is rekindled, where light is restored, and where covenant is rewritten daily.

Prophet Matthews' insights pierce through the silence that has crippled many marriages and relationships. His words echo the prophetic heart of God, declaring that even when blankets fall, when rings are lost, when voices grow silent, the Author of Love still whispers: "Do not cry—the story is not over." Love is an unfinished chapter, and with God, the pages are still being written.

I wholeheartedly commend this work to you. Read it not just with your mind, but with your spirit. Allow its truths to awaken you, to challenge you, and to call you higher. For in these pages lies a divine summons: to love as God loves, to communicate as heaven communicates, and to live a life of covenant not as an event, but as a daily prophetic reality.

Evangelist Dr. Gwen Marshall

Endorsement from Bishop Dr. Hurdis Bozeman

I extend my heartfelt congratulations to Dr. Laron Matthews, PhD, for this timely and powerful contribution to the body of Christ. As President of Global Evangelical Christian College and Seminary, I have had the privilege of witnessing Dr. Matthews commitment to excellence in both ministry and scholarship.

This book is yet another expression of that commitment. *Love: The Unfinished Chapter What Should've Been Told* is more than a testimony; it is a theological reflection grounded in Scripture and lived experience. Dr. Matthews speaks with the voice of a pastor, the wisdom of a counselor, and the authority of one who has walked through the valleys of life and emerged with faith intact. I believe this work will serve as a valuable resource for our students, churches, and communities worldwide. May it inspire readers to pursue love as God intended — enduring, sacrificial, and redemptive.

Bishop Dr. Hurdis Bozeman,

Global Evangelical Christian College and Seminary

Montgomery, Alabama

Endorsement from Dr. Samuel Hunter

Prophet Matthews has not simply written a book—he has crafted a time machine. Within these pages, men and women are invited to journey inward, to examine themselves honestly, and to measure the depth of their relationships. This book is more than words on paper; it is a mirror that reflects not only our relationships with our spouse or intended but also our covenant relationship with God.

As you read, you will be confronted with questions that challenge the heart: Am I still reaching for my spouse, or am I merely coexisting beside them? These pages uncover truths that many of us have overlooked. Love seldom departs suddenly. It doesn't slam the door, give a long goodbye, or vanish without warning. More often, it slips away slowly, quietly replaced by convenience, comfort, familiarity, and assumption.

Prophet Matthews leads us to recognize these shifts, not to condemn, but to restore. This book blesses us with deeper understanding—helping us to see clearly what has been lost, why it happened, and how to return. More than a reflection on human love, it guides us back to alignment with divine love, strengthening not only our marriages but also our walk with God.

Don't pass this by. If you allow it, this book will bring renewal to your home, your heart, and your spirit. Thank you Prophet Matthews, for being obedient to God's call and for sharing His message with courage and clarity. Truly, you are a prophet called to the nations, and this work is evidence of that calling.

Dr. Samuel Hunter

Pastoral Reflection from Bishop Milton Lee Seaborne Sr.

Prophet Dr. Laron Matthews Ph.D., is to witness a true embodiment of humble service and unwavering faith in our Lord and Savior, Jesus Christ. I had the privilege of first meeting him February 19th, 2021 at a church event in New Jersey. Since then, I have observed his remarkable spiritual growth and his steadfast commitment to both his personal walk with God and his leadership within the broader Christian community.

Dr. Matthews leads with clarity, conviction, and a profound sense of purpose—qualities that are clearly rooted in his deep love for Christ. His ministry reflects a consistent dedication to building, restoring, and empowering others through the Word of God.

This book is a powerful testament to that mission. It carries within its pages a life-changing and transformative message—one that will impact individuals and generations to come. It is more than just a book; it is a divinely inspired work that brings strength, hope, and spiritual renewal to all who engage with it.

Thank you, Dr. Laron Matthews, for your obedience in sharing this much-needed message of restoration. Your contribution to the body of Christ will undoubtedly bless and uplift countless lives.

Bishop Milton Lee Seaborne Sr

Global Deliverance Ministries of Jesus Christ International

Ministerial Endorsement from Dr. Marilyn Todman

It is with great honor and deep gratitude that I write this endorsement for *Love: The Unfinished Chapter – What Should've Been Told*. From the very first paragraph, it is clear that this work is not simply a book; it is a living message from the heart of God. Dr. Laron Matthews opens a sacred conversation about love, covenant, and restoration that our generation desperately needs to hear.

As a global media leader, I encounter stories every day—stories of triumph, stories of struggle, stories of love tested by time. Yet very few carry the prophetic weight and healing clarity that you will encounter in these pages. This book is a mirror and a roadmap. It reflects the hidden fractures that quietly weaken marriages, and it points us back to the altar where God alone can restore what life has tried to steal.

Dr. Matthews writes with a rare combination of courage and compassion. He speaks the unspoken and names the pain, but he never leaves the reader in despair. Instead, he invites us to rediscover the relentless love of God—a love that still covers, still heals, and still writes new chapters when we think the story is over. His words remind us that unfinished does not mean defeated, and that with Christ, every ending is a beginning waiting for grace.

To every husband and wife, every pastor, leader, and believer holding this book in your hands: read it with an open heart and an expectant spirit. Let it challenge you. Let it comfort you. Let it awaken the faith to fight for love—not just the romantic love that fades with time, but the covenant love that grows stronger through surrender.

Dr. Matthews, thank you for allowing God to use your life as both a testimony and a tool of transformation. This book is more than pages and ink; it is a prophetic call to rebuild the sacred walls of intimacy, honor, and trust.

May every reader find the courage to keep writing their own unfinished chapter with God as the Author, knowing that His love never fails and His story never ends.

With deep respect and joyful expectation,

Dr. Marilyn Todman

CEO & Founder, Preach The Word Worldwide Network Atlanta, Georgia

Acknowledgments

I would like to extend my deepest gratitude to all who have contributed to the journey of this book. To Bishop Zollie J. Keebler of House of Prayer, Prattville, AL, and Bishop Dr. Hurdis Bozeman of Global Evangelical Christian College and Seminary, Montgomery, AL, for their prayers, encouragement, and unwavering support. To Evangelist Dr. Gwen Marshall and Dr. Samuel Hunter for penning the forewords that frame this work with prophetic insight. To Administrator Retha Bryant of Laron Matthews Ministries, Montgomery, AL.

To my family, friends, and ministry partners who have stood with me in prayer and faith—thank you for believing in the mission of restoration, covenant, and love. This work would not be complete without your presence and your encouragement.

Dedication

This work is dedicated to the ministry family and to all those who seek to restore love, rebuild covenant, and walk faithfully with God. A special note of appreciation goes to Administrator Retha Bryant of Laron Matthews Ministries, whose unwavering dedication and administrative support continue to help carry this vision forward.

CHAPTER ONE

The Day the Blanket Fell Off the Bed

Scripture Focus

"For this reason a man shall leave his father and mother and be joined to his wife, and the two shall become one flesh."
— **Ephesians 5:31 (NKJV)**

There's a day in every marriage when something shifts—when comfort is uncovered, when what once covered you no longer does.

For me, it happened quietly. Not with an argument. Not with an affair. Not with fireworks.

It happened the day the blanket fell off the bed.

What once covered us—warmth, connection, intimacy—had slowly slipped away. And instead of pulling it back, we slept cold… separately… silently. It was a symbol of what our marriage had become.

The Bed Was Still There, But We Weren't in It Together

The bed didn't move. The sheets were still tucked. But something had changed—the spirit of the room was off. We were lying beside each other, but we were worlds apart.

It's one thing to be naked physically, but it's another to be uncovered emotionally, spiritually, and relationally.

We stopped reaching for the blanket—and more importantly, we stopped reaching for each other. And yet, that was the very place God called us to become one.

Uncovering Without Judgment

Genesis 2:25 says, *"They were both naked, the man and his wife, and were not ashamed."*

Before sin entered the world, nakedness was normal—vulnerability was sacred.

But today, many marriages struggle with spiritual nakedness because we fear being judged, rejected, or misunderstood. So we hide—not with fig leaves, but with silence, sarcasm, busyness, and routine.

But the day the blanket fell off the bed wasn't just a failure—it was an invitation.

God wasn't punishing me—He was showing me what we stopped protecting.

Our connection.

Our covenant.

Our covering.

When the Bedroom Becomes a Battleground

The place that once was our haven had become a hallway—just a space we passed through.

And that's the danger: we start treating sacred spaces as casual.

- We stop praying together.

- We stop talking after intimacy.

- We stop facing each other.

- We stop reaching for the blanket—and for each other.

But real marriage doesn't thrive in performance—it grows in presence.

And the bedroom isn't just for sex—it's for safety.

It's the place where wounds are seen and not mocked.

Where silence is shared, not feared.

Where two hearts, even cold, can still come back together under one covering.

God Re-Covers What We've Let Slip

Here's the hope: the blanket can be pulled back up.

What fell can be lifted.

What grew cold can be warmed again.

What slipped can be restored—*but only if we stop pretending it's still in place.*

I had to confess:

- I missed her.

- I missed us.

- I missed me—the man who used to reach for her, not just physically, but emotionally.

And as I spoke it, she reached too.

Sometimes healing doesn't start with fixing everything—it starts with pulling the blanket back up together.

Reflection Questions:

1. What have you stopped covering in your relationship?

    _____

    _____

    _____

    _____

2. Are you still reaching for your spouse — or just coexisting beside them?

    _____

    _____

    _____

    _____

3. Has your bed become a place of connection or avoidance?

    _____

    _____

    _____

    _____

4. How can you bring God back into your most intimate space?

    _____

    _____

    _____

    _____

Scripture Meditations:

- Ephesians 5:31–33

- Genesis 2:24–25

- 1 Corinthians 7:3–5

- Ecclesiastes 4:9–12

- Hebrews 13:4

CHAPTER TWO

When Love Turned Into Luxury

Scripture Focus

"You say, 'I am rich; I have acquired wealth and do not need a thing.' But you do not realize that you are wretched, pitiful, poor, blind and naked."
— **Revelation 3:17 (NIV)**

The Subtle Shift

Love didn't leave all at once. It didn't pack its bags, slam the door, or give a long goodbye. It left slowly—replaced by convenience, comfort, and assumption. At first, we called it *stability.* Then we called it *success.* But the truth was simple:

Our love turned into luxury.

We began to live next to each other, not with each other. We bought things to make our lives easier, but somewhere along the way, the marriage got harder. We upgraded the house, the car, the furniture—but not the connection. The relationship started to look better than it actually was.

We weren't arguing. We weren't broken. We were just… coasting.

Love Is Not a Purchase

There's a danger in material comfort. It makes you think you're okay. You eat well, you dress well, you smile in pictures. But the soul can still be starving. The marriage can still be dry.

We had nice sheets, but cold nights. A king-sized bed, but distance between us. I bought her gifts. She said thank you. But we stopped laughing the way we used to. We stopped praying together. We stopped fighting for us.

And I had to ask myself: Was I loving her, or just providing for her?

Love isn't proven by what you can buy—it's revealed in what you're willing to sacrifice. That's what Jesus showed us. He didn't give the Church diamonds. He gave His blood.

The Laodicea Lie

The church at Laodicea thought it had it all. Wealth, Image, Comfort. But in Revelation 3:17, Jesus speaks a hard truth:

You think you're rich—but you're actually poor.

That was us.

We thought we had matured. We thought the silence meant peace. But it was just spiritual apathy dressed up in a luxury lifestyle. We were physically close, emotionally distant, and spiritually blind.

That's what happens when love turns into luxury: you stop depending on God and start depending on stuff. You measure success by status. You count blessings by what you *have*, not who you are *becoming*.

Luxury Is Louder Than Love

The danger with luxury is that it talks louder than truth. It drowns out the whispers of the Holy Spirit. It gives the illusion of health while you're spiritually suffocating.

We had a big bed, but I stopped asking how her day was. We had smart TVs, but didn't look each other in the eyes. We traveled, but didn't touch each other's hearts. We took pictures, but never paused long enough to see each other's pain.

Luxury taught me how to live in comfort—but it also taught me how to live without her.

And that's when I knew something had to change.

Return to the Altar

I didn't need a new house. I needed a new heart. I needed to go back to the man I was when I first pursued her. When I prayed before every date. When I fasted for her healing. When I covered her in intercession and kissed her with intention.

Love turned into luxury—but luxury cannot sustain a marriage. Only the presence of God can.

So I asked God to strip me.

Not of my finances — but of my pride.

Of my performance.

Of my convenience.

I prayed like David, *"Restore to me the joy of Your salvation..."* (Psalm 51:12).

And when He did, I found her again.

Not just her body—but her soul.

The True Riches

Now I know: love thrives in humility. Love is loudest in the little things—the prayers no one sees, the apologies nobody demands, the forgiveness that costs everything.

True love doesn't live in luxury—it lives in the trenches.

In sickness and in health.

In the nights when nothing makes sense.

In the mornings when you still choose each other anyway.

The master bedroom is not about image. It's not about how well-decorated it is or how expensive the sheets are. It's about the covenant that lies within it—and the God who watches over it.

Love may have turned into luxury once.

But now, love is turning back into sacrifice.

Back into service.

Back into Him.

And that is the wealth I never want to lose again.

Reflection Questions:

1. Has comfort replaced your pursuit of intimacy with your spouse?

_____

_____

_____

_____

2. Are you loving from a place of sacrifice or performance?

_____

_____

_____

_____

3. What "luxuries" have replaced your hunger for connection?

_____

_____

_____

_____

4. How can you return to the altar — as a husband, as a man, as a servant?

_____

_____

_____

_____

Scripture Meditations:

- Revelation 3:14–22

- Ephesians 5:2

- Matthew 6:21

- Psalm 51:10–12

CHAPTER THREE

The 911 Next to Me

Scripture Focus

"My beloved put his hand by the latch of the door, and my heart yearned for him...
I opened for my beloved, but my beloved had turned away and was gone."
— **Song of Solomon 5:4, 6 (NKJV)**

Sleeping Beside an Emergency

I was lying in bed one night, thinking about my next move, my next project, my next check. And right beside me, my wife was crying. Quietly. Silently. Her back was turned, her body was still, but her soul was screaming.

And I didn't hear it.

I didn't ask.

I didn't roll over.

I didn't pray.

That night, I slept next to a 911 call and didn't even dial in. That was the night I realized: it is possible to share a bed with someone and not share their burden. To be physically close but emotionally absent. To have no clue that the person who lies next to you every night is in crisis.

Married But Missing

You don't have to be gone to be absent. You can be present in body and completely detached in spirit. That's the dangerous part of routine—it numbs your sensitivity. It turns moments of ministry into moments of maintenance. And before long, your wife becomes a roommate. Your bedroom becomes a battleground of silence.

She smiled at the dinner table. She served the children. She ironed my clothes. But she was unraveling inside.

And I didn't notice.

Song of Solomon 5 shows the Shulamite woman waking up to respond to her husband's approach—but by the time she opened the door, he was gone. What a painful picture. She was willing, but he had already left. How many times have we emotionally exited before giving our wives a chance to speak?

The Call You Didn't Answer

Every marriage has a silent emergency at some point—those unspoken needs, those hidden frustrations, those moments when your spouse is crying for help in a language you've stopped listening to.

And let me be honest: I wasn't cruel. I wasn't intentionally ignoring her. I was just distracted. By ministry. By work. By the idea that as long as there's no argument, everything must be fine.

But *fine* is a lie when you stop checking in.

We check the oil in our cars. We check our bank accounts. We check social media. But we don't always check our wives' hearts. When's the last time you asked her how her spirit is doing—not just her schedule?

You don't need to be a paramedic to recognize a 911. You just need to be present.

The Ministry of Attention

Jesus noticed the woman who touched the hem of His garment. He turned around in a crowd to find her. That's what love does— it notices. It stops. It listens. It responds.

As husbands, we are not just providers—we are responders. And sometimes the call isn't loud. Sometimes the 911 doesn't come with sirens—it comes with silence. With withdrawal. With eyes that no longer shine. With smiles that no longer reach the soul.

I had to repent for not seeing her. For not hearing what she wasn't saying. For letting my busyness become blindness. And in my repentance, I learned something:

You can't fix what you don't acknowledge.

And you can't acknowledge what you refuse to notice.

She Was Waiting

That night, I turned over. I asked her, "Are you okay?" It was a simple question—one I should've asked sooner. She paused, then said something I'll never forget:

"I've been waiting for you to see me."

That broke me.

She had been waving the flag of her fatigue. Carrying burdens with a brave face. Crying in the shower, smiling in public. All while I lay inches away—unaware.

God had placed a 911 next to me, and I almost missed it.

God's Wake-Up Call

This chapter of our love story taught me that true love is not just felt—it's noticed. It's responsive. It's tuned in. The master bedroom is not just for rest or romance—it's a place of discernment. A place where you should hear what's not being said. Feel what's not being touched. And answer the call before it turns into silence.

Brothers, your wife's silence is not peace. Her distance is not rebellion. It may be a 911—a spiritual emergency—waiting for your voice, your presence, your leadership.

Be the man who turns over.

Be the husband who checks in.

Be the priest who answers the call.

Because sometimes, the greatest emergency is the one lying right next to you.

Reflection Questions:

1. Are you aware of your spouse's emotional or spiritual needs right now?

_____

_____

_____

_____

2. Have you mistaken routine for peace in your marriage?

_____

_____

_____

_____

3. What signs have you missed that your spouse may be struggling?

_____

_____

_____

_____

4. How can you become more spiritually responsive as a husband?

_____

_____

_____

_____

Scripture Meditations:

- Song of Solomon 5:2–8

- 1 Peter 3:7

- Philippians 2:4

- Proverbs 20:5

CHAPTER FOUR

When the Pillow Talk Ended

Scripture Focus

"Death and life are in the power of the tongue, and those who love it will eat its fruit."
— **Proverbs 18:21 (NKJV)**

The Silence After the Softness

There was a time when the pillow was sacred.

It was the altar where we laid our hearts bare. After the day was done, after the house grew quiet, it was there—on that cotton-covered confession booth—that we whispered our hopes, laughed about little things, and planned our future. That was our time.

But one night, I rolled over and realized the pillow talk had ended.

No more whispered prayers.

No more giggles in the dark.

No more, *"Tell me how your day really went."*

Just silence.

Cold, clean silence.

And I knew—we were speaking less because we were feeling less. Not because we didn't care, but because we had stopped cultivating.

Pillow Talk Was the Pulse

In marriage, pillow talk is like a pulse. It lets you know your connection is still beating. It's not the deep conversations that prove intimacy—it's the consistent ones. The everyday check-ins, the "you good?" moments, the "I miss you and you're lying right here" confessions. That's where hearts stay alive.

But when those moments stop, disconnection begins—not with arguments, but with absence. The absence of affection. The absence of pursuit. The absence of voice.

Pillow talk doesn't die because of one storm. It dies because of consistent neglect.

The Ministry of a Whisper

God rarely shouts. He speaks in stillness. In whispers. In soft places. That's why the enemy loves noise—because noise drowns out the divine. In the same way, the master bedroom was never meant to be a courtroom—it was meant to be a sanctuary. A place of soft voices and sacred trust.

But we had filled it with everything else. Work, Worry, Screens, Fatigue and eventually… silence.

The same bed that once held our laughter now held unspoken questions.

And I realized something: You can't share a bed without sharing your heart. That's not a marriage—that's a performance.

Why Did It Stop?

I asked myself, *"When did we stop talking?"*

It wasn't all at once. It was gradual. A few busy nights. A few distracted evenings. A few too-tired-to-talk moments. Then it became normal. Then it became acceptable. Then it became dangerous.

The most dangerous silence is the one that feels normal.

I didn't stop loving her—I just stopped expressing it. I assumed she knew. I assumed she felt it. But love, when left unspoken, feels uncertain. Love that is never heard becomes love eventually questioned.

Even God speaks daily. His Word says His mercies are new every morning (Lamentations 3:22–23). He keeps talking—even when we stop listening.

So why had I stopped talking to the one I vowed to love?

What Happens Without Words

When pillow talk ends, assumptions begin.

She assumes I don't care.

I assume she's distant.

She wonders what happened to us.

I wonder if she's still interested.

And all the while, we both want the same thing—to be seen, heard, pursued. But pride gets in the way. Fatigue gets in the way. Silence becomes our unspoken agreement.

But silence is a seed. And whatever you plant will grow.

Reigniting the Soft Place

One night, I turned to her and whispered, "I miss this."

She looked at me. Her eyes filled—not with tears, but with relief. I wasn't the only one who noticed. I wasn't the only one who missed the sound of our love.

We didn't start with deep talks. We just started again.

"How was your heart today?"

"What are you afraid of right now?"

"What can I pray for?"

It wasn't loud. It wasn't long. But it was healing.

The pillow became a sanctuary again.

And God met us there.

Words Heal What Hands Can't Reach

I learned that intimacy starts with conversation. Sex without communication is performance. But a whisper of love, a sentence of affirmation, a pause to listen—those are the things that keep covenant alive.

Brothers, talk to her. Not because there's a problem. Talk because there's a promise. Let the bedroom be filled with more than just silence or stress. Fill it with gentle words, with laughter, with questions, with dreams. Let her know you still want her—her thoughts, her prayers, her voice.

Because when the pillow talk ends, disconnection begins. But when it returns, so does the love.

Reflection Questions:

1. When was the last time you and your spouse had meaningful pillow talk?

_____

_____

_____

_____

2. What distractions have taken over your nighttime connection?

_____

_____

_____

_____

3. Have you allowed silence to become normal in your marriage?

_____

_____

_____

_____

4. What one question can you ask tonight to open the conversation again?

_____

_____

_____

_____

Scripture Meditations:

- Proverbs 18:21

- Song of Solomon 2:14

- James 1:19

- Lamentations 3:22–23

CHAPTER FIVE

The Position I Once Loved, Now I Like It

Scripture Focus

*"Let your fountain be blessed, and rejoice in the wife of
your youth.
As a loving deer and a graceful doe, let her breasts satisfy you
at all times;
and always be enraptured with her love."*
— **Proverbs 5:18–19 (NKJV)**

From Passion to Pattern

There was a time when just the thought of her stirred something
in me. Not just physically, but emotionally. Spiritually. I didn't
just want her body—I longed for her soul. The sound of her voice.
The way she prayed. The scent she left on my shirt.

Everything about her was a pursuit.

But something happened.

We got comfortable. We got predictable. We found a rhythm—
and we stayed there.

One day, I realized: the position I once loved, I now just like. It still brought pleasure. It still brought release. But it didn't carry the same wonder. The same fire. The same worship.

And that's when I knew—I had started to treat a holy thing like a habit.

The Sacredness of Intimacy

God created intimacy between a husband and wife not just for reproduction or relief, but for reconnection. It's covenant activity. It's sacred warfare. It's worship in the form of oneness.

But routine can become a silent thief. What started as holy can become hollow. The moment becomes more about function than fellowship.

It wasn't just about positions in the bedroom. It was about posture in the heart.

We were still "performing," but not pursuing.

Still "touching," but not treasuring.

Still "available," but not vulnerable.

The master bedroom became a place of physical unity without spiritual intimacy. And I started asking God, *"Where did the love go?"*

Love Is More Than Like

In Revelation 2, Jesus rebukes the church at Ephesus. He tells them they've done many good things—but they've left their first love. That was us.

We were still committed. Still monogamous. Still faithful. But we had left our first love—that raw, reckless, tender pursuit of one another.

I didn't fall out of love with her. I just started liking her more than I loved her. I became content with the familiar. Satisfied with the routine. But love doesn't settle—it chases. It refreshes. It relearns.

When you only *like* something, you tolerate changes. When you *love* something, you fight to revive it.

Fighting Familiarity

Familiarity is the enemy of fire. You stop seeing what you once marveled at. You stop noticing the curve of her smile or the weight she carries in her silence. You stop pursuing her prayers. You stop seeing her as a gift and start seeing her as an obligation.

That's how the position becomes predictable. The passion fades not because the body changed, but because the pursuit stopped.

And let me say this to every man reading: If you're bored, it's not her body that needs changing—it's your eyes that need renewing. God doesn't need to change your wife to revive your desire. He just needs to change your heart.

When Desire Is Reborn

I asked God to help me see her again. To remove the layers of stress, routine, and assumption. To strip away the lust from outside and restore the love within.

And something shifted.

I started looking at her the way I used to—as the answer to my prayers. As the one I fasted for. The one I couldn't stop thinking about. The one I vowed to protect, pursue, and please.

We didn't need new positions—we needed renewed passion. We didn't need new techniques—we needed new tenderness.

And when that came, the fire came back.

Intimacy Is a Ministry

God showed me that my role as a husband in the bedroom isn't to perform—it's to minister. To meet her where she is. To hold her soul while holding her body. To speak life into her even in the most vulnerable moments.

The position I once loved, I now love again—not because it's new, but because I showed up differently.

And that's the lesson: It's not about changing the physical. It's about renewing the spiritual. When your heart changes, the same old position becomes a new place of passion again.

Reflection Questions:

1. Have you mistaken routine for intimacy in your marriage?

_____

_____

_____

_____

2. What areas of your love life have become familiar instead of sacred?

_____

_____

_____

_____

3. Are you ministering to your spouse or just "performing"?

_____

_____

_____

_____

4. What would it look like to pursue your spouse like you did in the beginning?

_____

_____

_____

_____

Scripture Meditations:

- Proverbs 5:15–19

- Song of Solomon 7:6–10

- Revelation 2:4–5

- 1 Corinthians 7:3–5

CHAPTER SIX

Who Turned the Light Off in the Room

Scripture Focus

*"The spirit of a man is the lamp of the Lord,
searching all the inner depths of his heart."*
— **Proverbs 20:27 (NKJV)**

The Day the Room Went Dim

There wasn't a flicker. No dramatic moment. Just darkness.

One night, I walked into our bedroom, and I could feel it—the light was off. Not just the bulb above us, but the warmth between us. The joy that once danced in her eyes was gone. The air was heavier. Something sacred had dimmed.

We weren't mad. We weren't yelling. But something was missing.

And I asked myself, *Who turned the light off in this room?*

When the Glow Fades

In the early days of love, everything glows. The laughter lights up the night. The touch, the timing, the tone—it's all radiant. But then life starts to weigh in. Disappointments come. Words are spoken and not forgotten. Prayers go unanswered. And slowly, the glow fades.

Not because the love is gone—but because the light source shifted.

We were still functioning as a couple. Still doing the duties. Still lying in the same bed. But the spiritual current wasn't flowing. We had stopped praying together. Stopped checking in. Stopped repenting. Stopped reflecting.

And without even knowing it, the room went dark.

Light Comes from Within

Proverbs tells us that the spirit of a man is the lamp of the Lord. That means real light in a marriage doesn't come from candles or compliments—it comes from connection with God. If we stop feeding our spirit, we stop shining.

I thought the issue was her mood. Or her distance. Or our routine. But the real issue was that I had stopped being the lamp. I had stopped leading in the Spirit. Stopped initiating prayer. Stopped reading the Word with her. Stopped washing her with the water of the Word (Ephesians 5:26).

And when the man goes dark, the room soon follows.

The Darkness We Don't Talk About

No one teaches you how to handle spiritual darkness in marriage. We talk about conflict, infidelity, finances—but not the silence that creeps in when God's presence is no longer prioritized.

We became excellent at pretending. Good at smiling in public. Skilled at working in ministry. But in the private place—in the bedroom, where intimacy meets spirituality—we were cold. Dim. Disconnected.

And here's what I learned: Darkness doesn't just rob you of passion—it robs you of *purpose*. The master bedroom is where vision is spoken. Where restoration happens. Where unity is sealed. And when the light goes out there, everything else starts to unravel.

Who Turned the Light Off?

The truth? I did.

Not with one decision, but with many small ones:

- When I chose to scroll instead of listen.
- When I held offense instead of giving grace.
- When I stopped initiating our devotions.
- When I let fatigue replace prayer.
- When I ignored the Spirit's nudging to say, "I'm sorry."

Turning off the light doesn't require a blowout—just a slow, steady neglect of what matters.

Turning the Light Back On

But here's the good news: Light comes quickly to the humble.

One night, I simply said, "Let's pray."

It wasn't long. I didn't try to be deep. I just held her hand and said, "God, come back into this room."

And something shifted.

She cried.

I cried.

Because light doesn't just reveal—it heals. It showed us how far we'd drifted, and how near God still was.

We didn't need therapy that night.

We needed light.

And light came when the Spirit was invited back in.

Let the Man Light the Flame

As husbands, we carry a spiritual responsibility. We are the priests of our homes. That means we are not just protectors—we are igniters. Our pursuit of God fuels the light in the room. Our worship opens the windows of heaven. Our repentance softens the spiritual atmosphere.

And when we stop burning, the bedroom turns cold.

It's not about lighting candles or saying all the right things. It's about letting the fire of God return to the place where your covenant breathes.

This Room Still Has a Light

If your bedroom has grown cold…

If the talks have stopped…

If the passion has dulled…

If the spiritual pulse has slowed…

Don't just buy roses.

Don't just book vacations.

Turn the light back on.

Pray together.

Repent together.

Worship together.

Let the Holy Spirit invade that room again—because what darkness took, light can restore in an instant.

Reflection Questions:

1. Has your marriage bed become more functional than spiritual?

_____

_____

_____

_____

2. When was the last time you and your spouse prayed together in your bedroom?

_____

_____

_____

_____

3. What daily habits have slowly turned the light off in your relationship?

_____

_____

_____

_____

4. What does turning the light back on look like for you today?

_____

_____

_____

_____

Scripture Meditations:

- Proverbs 20:27

- Matthew 5:14–16

- Ephesians 5:8–14

- 1 Peter 3:7

- Genesis 1:3 – "Let there be light"

CHAPTER SEVEN

Who Turned the Light On in the Room

Scripture Focus

"Arise, shine; for your light has come!
And the glory of the Lord is risen upon you."
— **Isaiah 60:1 (NKJV)**

When the Room Lit Up Again

It didn't happen with a switch.

It didn't happen with a song.

It happened in a moment of surrender.

I had grown so used to the dimness that when the light finally came back on, it startled me. It didn't come through loud praise or passionate kisses. It came when I humbled myself and whispered, *"God, we need You in this room again."*

And like dawn breaking through a weary night, the room filled with warmth again.

Not just warmth from her skin, but warmth from His Spirit.

This time, the light didn't come from the lamp—it came from within us.

The Light Was Never Gone — We Just Stopped Looking

Looking back, I now know the light was never really gone. We had just closed our eyes to it. Covered it with distractions. Dimmed it with pride. Buried it under busyness.

But God's presence never truly left—we just stopped inviting it in.

And all it took to restore it was one decision: to be open again.

Open to healing.

Open to honest conversation.

Open to forgiveness.

Open to rediscovering each other—not as roles or responsibilities, but as souls in covenant.

Light Doesn't Just Illuminate — It Revives

When light comes into a room, it reveals what was hidden. It shows you what needs cleaning. But more than that—it revives what was dying.

That night, when the light came back on, we didn't just see each other again. We saw God's hand on us.

We saw:

- Grace over our failures.

- Strength for our weaknesses.

- Beauty in our brokenness.

- Hope in our silence.

It was as if the Spirit whispered, *"This room still has purpose. This bed still carries power. This marriage is still Mine."*

Light Brings Accountability

When the light comes on, you can't hide anymore.

You can't pretend everything's okay.

You can't mask pain with routine.

And that's the beauty of it—the light doesn't shame you. It restores you. It calls you back to truth. To intentionality. To spiritual leadership.

For the first time in a long time, I saw her clearly. Not just her figure, but her fight. Not just her position in my life, but her pain in our silence.

And in that moment, I repented—not just to her, but to God.

Men, Be the Light

The Lord reminded me: *You are the light-bearer.*

Not because I'm perfect, but because I'm positioned.

God has called the man to be the head—and with that calling comes responsibility. We don't just turn on lights by what we say—we turn them on by how we live.

When we walk in integrity, the room lights up.

When we speak life over her, the room lights up.

When we honor her in private, the room lights up.

When we cover her in prayer, the room lights up.

You want the fire back? Don't just touch her body—touch heaven on her behalf. Let your spirit be the lamp that keeps the room lit, even when life tries to dim it.

The Light Revealed the New Us

After the light came on, things didn't go back to normal—and thank God for that.

We weren't trying to relive old memories—we were building new ones. We weren't chasing old sparks—we were discovering deeper fire.

The intimacy grew deeper.

The prayers grew stronger.

The smiles lasted longer.

And the bed—once cold and quiet—became a sanctuary again.

Not because we figured it all out.

But because we let the Light in.

Reflection Questions:

1. What would it look like to intentionally bring spiritual light into your marriage?

_____

_____

_____

_____

2. Are there areas of your relationship still hiding in the dark?

_____

_____

_____

_____

3. Have you assumed the light was gone when God was simply waiting for surrender?

_____

_____

_____

_____

4. How can you, as a husband, lead your home into the light today?

_____

_____

_____

_____

Scripture Meditations:

- Isaiah 60:1

- Ephesians 5:8–14

- John 1:5

- Matthew 5:14–16

- Psalm 119:105

CHAPTER EIGHT

Who Stained the Sheets

Scripture Focus

*"Though your sins are like scarlet,
they shall be as white as snow;
though they are red like crimson,
they shall be as wool."*
— **Isaiah 1:18 (NKJV)**

The Evidence Was There

I remember looking down and seeing it — a stain that didn't belong. Not just a mark on the fabric, but something deeper. A symbol. A sign. A reminder that something sacred had been violated.

The sheets told a story we weren't saying out loud.

It wasn't just a physical issue — it was emotional, spiritual, and relational.

Something had seeped into the sacred and left behind a mark.

And like Adam and Eve in the garden, we tried to cover it.

But the truth about stained sheets is this: no matter how you flip them, you always know where the spot is.

Hidden Marks in Holy Places

In marriage, the bed is not just a place of intimacy — it's a place of covenant. When we say *"for better or worse,"* we invite God into that space. But when sin enters — through betrayal, lust, secrets, silence, bitterness, or emotional distance — the sheets get stained.

Maybe it wasn't infidelity.

Maybe it was:

- The lies that stacked up.
- The conversations that shouldn't have happened.
- The fantasies entertained alone at night.
- The bitterness soaking the fabric of fellowship.

Stains don't always scream.

Sometimes they soak — quietly, slowly — until the cloth is no longer clean.

Who Did It? Who Let It Happen?

The question isn't just, *"What happened?"* It's, *"Who stained the sheets?"*

Was it my pride?

Her silence?

The distance we never discussed?

The content we allowed into our eyes and ears?

The vow I failed to protect in a moment of weakness?

I wanted to justify. To minimize. To point the finger.

But the Spirit whispered, *"Start with you."*

So I did.

Confession Is the First Step Toward Clean

One of the hardest things for a man to do is confess — not just to his wife, but to God. To admit he let something holy become defiled. To say:

"Yes, Lord... I stained what You made sacred."

But here is the hope:

God doesn't shame — He cleanses.

Isaiah promises that though our sins are scarlet, God will make them white as snow.

That includes sheets.

That includes hearts.

That includes marriages that feel too damaged to redeem.

The key is not hiding the stain — it's confessing it.

Because hidden stains create lasting pain.

She Saw It Too

I thought I was carrying it alone.

But when I finally brought it up, she said:

"I knew something had changed. I just didn't know how to say it."

She saw the stain.

She felt it in my distance.

In my eyes avoiding hers.

In the way I turned over instead of turning toward her.

Stains create silence.

Silence builds walls.

But once we talked — really talked — healing began.

Not because we had solutions, but because we had honesty.

The God Who Washes Sheets

God reminded me of something powerful:

He still washes feet — and He still washes sheets.

He can cleanse what we've soiled.

He can sanctify what we've sullied.

He can redeem what we regret.

But only if we invite Him in.

So we did.

We sat in that room, held those same sheets, and prayed:

"Lord, let Your blood wash this room clean."

And He did.

Covering vs. Cleansing

There's a difference between covering a stain and cleansing it.

- **Covering** is driven by shame.

- **Cleansing** is driven by grace.

Covering says, *"Don't let anyone see this."*

Cleansing says, *"Lord, heal what's already been seen."*

Many couples keep changing the linens… but never address why they're dirty.

Don't Throw the Bed Away

We almost did.

The thought crossed my mind:

"Let's buy a new set. Move. Start fresh. Replace everything that reminds us of this."

But the Lord said:

"I don't want you to replace the bed — I want to redeem it."

And in the same place where pain entered, healing began.

Because the same God who saw the stain is the same God who removes it with His love.

Reflection Questions:

1. Are there "stains" in your marriage that have gone unspoken?

   _____

   _____

   _____

   _____

2. Have you been trying to hide or cover up what only God can cleanse?

   _____

   _____

   _____

   _____

3. What would honest confession look like in your marriage right now?

   _____

   _____

   _____

   _____

4. Do you believe God can restore even the most stained places of intimacy?

   _____

   _____

   _____

   _____

Scripture Meditations:

- Isaiah 1:18
- Psalm 51:7–12
- 1 John 1:9
- Hebrews 13:4
- Ephesians 5:25–27

CHAPTER NINE

When the Rings Got Lost

Scripture Focus

"He remembers His covenant forever, the word which He commanded, for a thousand generations." — ***Psalm 105:8 (NKJV)***

The Ring Was Just Metal — Until It Went Missing

It was just a ring.

Until the day it wasn't there.

I looked down at my hand and felt an emptiness I didn't expect. I had taken it off before — at the gym, in the kitchen, while cleaning. But this time… I couldn't find it.

And suddenly, that small band of metal felt heavier than it ever had.

Because it wasn't about the ring itself.

It was about what it represented:

The covenant. The commitment. The calling.

And in that moment I realized — we had lost more than jewelry.

When Symbols Fade, So Do Standards

Marriage rings are symbolic, yes — but they're also a standard.

They say to the world:

"I belong to someone."

"I am in covenant."

But when the ring gets lost and no one is urgent about finding it... that's when the heart starts wandering.

In many marriages, the rings are still worn, but the meaning has faded.

- The vows have dulled.
- The passion has slipped.
- The priorities have shifted.

We stop holding hands.

We stop checking in.

We stop saying *"I love you"* and start just going through the motions.

And one day, without even noticing, we lose the ring in our hearts — not just the one on our finger.

The Real Loss Wasn't the Ring — It Was the Reverence

As I sat on the edge of the bed that night, I asked myself:

"When did I stop protecting what was sacred?"

The missing ring was just a symptom.

The deeper loss was the slow erosion of honor.

Neglect had crept in:

- Missed moments.

- Small dishonors.

- Drift disguised as routine.

- Carelessness where covenant should've been guarded.

When reverence leaves a marriage, rings don't mean much.

We didn't plan to lose anything.

But neglect steals what intentionality protects.

God Never Misplaces His Covenant

Here's the beautiful truth of the gospel:

We may lose sight of covenant — but God never does.

Even when we drift, He remembers.

Even when we forget the ring, He remembers the vow.

His covenant is rooted not in our consistency, but in His character.

That is the model for marriage:

Not just ring-wearing, but covenant-keeping.

Weeks later, when I finally found the ring — tucked away in the most unexpected place — it was scratched and worn... but still whole.

And the Spirit whispered:

"That's your marriage.

Not perfect.

Not untouched.

But still standing.

Still worth wearing.

Still worth honoring."

When We Lost the Rings, We Found the Reason

Strangely, losing the rings was what helped us rediscover the meaning behind them.

We talked about why they mattered.

We talked about what we were truly missing — not metal, but meaning.

There was no grand ceremony.

No audience.

No fanfare.

Just the two of us, in the sacred quiet of our bedroom.

We took each other's hands and lifted them to heaven:

"Lord, restore the covenant.

Restore the honor.

Restore the joy."

And He did.

Not because we found the ring.

But because we found remembrance.

The Ring Is a Reminder — Not the Root

A ring doesn't make you faithful.

But honoring the covenant does.

When your heart is anchored in God's Word, the ring becomes more than jewelry — it becomes a living reminder of grace, endurance, forgiveness, and unconditional love.

So if the rings have been lost — physically or symbolically — don't just replace them.

Restore the reason you wore them in the first place.

Because covenant is the real treasure.

And God is still able to redeem what was misplaced.

Reflection Questions:

1. Have you ever felt like you "lost the ring" emotionally or spiritually, even while still wearing it?

_____

_____

_____

_____

2. What does your wedding band mean to you now compared to when you first put it on?

_____

_____

_____

_____

3. How can you restore reverence for the covenant you made before God?

_____

_____

_____

_____

4. In what areas has neglect crept into your relationship?

_____

_____

_____

_____

Scripture Meditations:

- Matthew 19:6

- Ecclesiastes 4:12

- Hosea 2:19–20

- Malachi 2:15–16

- Romans 11:29 – "For the gifts and the calling of God are irrevocable."

CHAPTER TEN

When the Seed Stopped Working and the Egg Started Wondering

Scripture Focus

"He gives the childless woman a family, making her a happy mother. Praise the Lord!" — **Psalm 113:9 (NLT)**

When Fruitfulness Was Our Expectation

Marriage carried us into the sacred chamber not only for connection, but for creation. We believed — with every intimate moment and every whispered prayer — that God would bless our union with fruit.

The seed would do what it was designed to do.

The egg would receive what it was formed to carry.

Life would come forth.

But then time passed.

And the womb remained silent.

And questions started whispering louder than our faith.

The Silence in the Bedroom

The silence wasn't just physical.

It was emotional.

Spiritual.

Heavy.

Month after month.

Prayer after prayer.

Test after test.

And still... nothing.

I began questioning my manhood.

She began questioning her purpose.

Together, we started questioning God's plan.

And somewhere in the ache, the seed stopped working — not just biologically, but spiritually. My confidence as a husband shrank. Her joy as a wife dimmed. And in the shadows of disappointment, the egg — the hope, the dream, the expectation — began to wonder:

Why hasn't it happened?

Did we do something wrong?

Is this punishment — or pruning?

Are we still "one" if we can't produce "two"?

God Is Still God — Even When the Womb Waits

We had to learn — painfully — that God is not obligated to move according to our timetable.

Fruitfulness in His eyes is deeper than producing children.

It's faith.

It's perseverance.

It's worship without results.

Scripture is filled with barren places that God blessed anyway:

- Sarah laughed — yet conceived Isaac.
- Hannah wept bitterly — yet birthed Samuel.
- Elizabeth carried shame — yet delivered John.

God still opens what man calls closed.

And more than that — He heals what man calls broken.

When Desire Becomes Division

Infertility didn't just test our biology — it tested our bond.

We had to fight to stay *with* each other, not just *beside* each other.

Because when you're hurting, it's easy to isolate.

Easy to blame.

Easy to feel "less than."

And that's exactly where the enemy wants a marriage — divided in the very place where unity is needed most.

I stopped initiating.

She stopped responding.

We stopped dreaming.

But praise God — we never stopped praying.

Even when the prayers were short.

Even when the tears did the speaking.

Even when fatigue was stronger than faith.

What If the Seed Was Never Just Sperm?

One night in prayer, the Lord whispered to my spirit:

"What if the seed I care most about is not physical, but spiritual?"

That question broke something open in me.

I realized the seed wasn't only biology — it was responsibility.

My leadership.

My love.

My integrity.

My covering as a husband.

I couldn't control the outcome of conception — but I *could* control the soil of our marriage.

I could still sow tenderness.

Speak life.

Water her soul with grace.

Believe that God was producing something eternal, even if invisible.

When the Egg Wonders, the Word Must Anchor

My wife once whispered through tears, "I don't know if it's ever going to happen for us."

And I didn't answer with clichés.

I answered with covenant:

"God never promised us children the way we imagined. But He did promise us purpose. And whatever comes — or doesn't come — we still win if we stay faithful."

That night, something shifted.

The egg — that fragile, trembling hope — rested again.

Not because certainty came, but because truth did.

There Is Life Beyond the Womb

Eventually, we learned that life isn't measured only in the babies you birth — but in the people you become.

- Becoming stronger.
- Becoming closer.
- Becoming surrendered.
- Becoming a testimony to others walking through silent battles.

Some couples will conceive biologically.

Others will adopt, foster, or raise spiritual sons and daughters.

But **all** can be fruitful — *if they remain faithful.*

Because fruitfulness is not defined by reproduction. It's defined by obedience.

Reflection Questions:

1. Have you equated your value or manhood/womanhood with your ability to produce?

   _____

   _____

   _____

   _____

2. How has disappointment impacted your connection with your spouse?

   _____

   _____

   _____

   _____

3. Are you allowing the Word of God to anchor your identity during seasons of delay or barrenness?

   _____

   _____

   _____

   _____

4. What fruit is God producing in your marriage beyond the physical?

   _____

   _____

   _____

   _____

Scripture Meditations:

- Psalm 113:9

- Genesis 18:14

- 1 Samuel 1:10–20

- Luke 1:36–37

- John 15:5

CHAPTER ELEVEN

The Day I Became Impotent

Scripture Focus

"My grace is sufficient for you, for My strength is made perfect in weakness." — **2 Corinthians 12:9 (NKJV)**

It Wasn't Just My Body That Failed

The day I became impotent wasn't really about what happened in my body.

Yes — something changed physically.

The strength I once relied on… failed.

The passion that once came easily… flickered.

The performance I quietly took pride in… slipped.

But deeper than the diagnosis was the unraveling of identity.

I didn't just lose function — **I felt like I lost manhood.**

I wasn't just weak in flesh — **I was broken in spirit.**

And sitting in that reality, I asked myself a painful question:

"Who am I now?"

More Than a Bedroom Issue

For many men, the word *impotent* carries shame.

But this wasn't just about intimacy — it was about insecurity.

It showed up in the way I prayed.

In the way I walked through the house.

In the way I avoided my wife's eyes.

In the way I questioned my worth as a husband.

The true impotence wasn't just physical — **it was emotional and spiritual.**

Somewhere along the journey, I had tied my masculinity to performance... instead of purpose.

God Had to Break What I Built Without Him

I built an image of manhood that was more *cultural* than *biblical*:

- Always strong.
- Always ready.
- Always in control.
- Always able.

But God had a different blueprint.

He allowed what I leaned on to fail — not to humiliate me, but to **liberate me.**

To show me:

- True manhood isn't about performance — but presence.

- Not about control — but covering.
- Not about ability — but accountability to the One who gives strength.

God had to break the version of "manhood" I built… so He could rebuild me according to His design.

When She Held Me Without Expecting Me

I'll never forget the night I broke down.

Not from pain.

From pressure.

I couldn't be "that man" anymore — the perfect husband, the unshakable rock, the strong one who always had the answers.

But she didn't pull away.

She didn't accuse.

She didn't question my worth.

She held me.

Not with disappointment.

Not with frustration.

Just **love**.

No expectations.

Just presence.

And in her arms, I saw the heart of God — not through performance restored, but through *relationship redeemed.*

Sometimes God doesn't restore you with results — **He restores you with reassurance.**

God Can Still Use Impotent Men

Scripture is full of men who lacked physical power — yet carried divine purpose.

- **Abraham** was impotent, yet became father of nations.
- **Moses** stuttered, yet led millions to freedom.
- **Paul** carried a thorn, yet built churches and wrote Scripture.

Their limitations never limited God.

Your weakness does not cancel your calling.

Your failure does not void your future.

In fact — **your inability may be the platform where God displays His greatest strength.**

Redefining Strength in the Light of Grace

I stopped begging God for function… and started seeking Him for faithfulness.

I prayed:

- "Restore my mind before my body."
- "Strengthen my love before my libido."
- "Grow my endurance before my excitement."

And day by day, God rebuilt me — not into the man I used to be, but into the man I was meant to become:

- A man defined by presence, not pressure.

- A husband defined by love, not performance.
- A vessel defined by surrender, not strength.

There's Grace for That Too

If you're a man walking through the quiet pain of feeling "less than," hear this:

There is grace for you.

God does not abandon broken men.

He meets them in their weakness.

He reminds them:

"My grace is sufficient. My strength is made perfect in your weakness."

The day I became impotent was the day God exposed my dependence on myself... and invited me to depend on Him.

And now?

I'm more of a man than I've ever been — not because of what I can do, but because of what **He** is doing in me.

Reflection Questions:

1. Have you ever tied your identity to your physical or emotional performance?

_____

_____

_____

_____

2. How do you respond when your strength fails?

_____

_____

_____

_____

3. Is your definition of manhood rooted in Scripture or in culture?

_____

_____

_____

_____

4. How can you invite God into your weakness and allow Him to redefine your worth?

_____

_____

_____

_____

Scripture Meditations:

- 2 Corinthians 12:9

- Romans 4:19–21

- Isaiah 40:29–31

- 1 Peter 5:6–7

- Philippians 1:6

CHAPTER TWELVE

The Ceremony Is Over

Scripture Focus

"Unless the Lord builds the house, they labor in vain who build it." — **Psalm 127:1 (NKJV)**

The Aisle Was Beautiful — But It Wasn't a Guarantee

The ceremony was flawless.

The flowers were fresh.

The tux was clean.

The vows were strong.

The guests cried and clapped as we said *"I do."*

But then…

The music stopped.

The guests went home.

The photographer packed up.

The lights dimmed.

And all that remained was **us** — two people, staring at a future that suddenly felt very different without the filter of celebration.

The ceremony was over.

Now the covenant would be tested.

When Marriage Feels Like a Performance That Has Ended

There comes a moment in every relationship when the stage lights dim and the reality of covenant sets in.

No more rehearsed vows.

No more applause.

No more perfectly timed pictures.

Just:

- Silence
- Bills
- Exhaustion
- Miscommunication
- Disappointment
- Decisions

And in that raw space, it's easy to feel like the marriage ended when the music ended.

But the truth?

The real marriage had just begun.

The Difference Between the Promise and the Process

A ceremony is built on promises.

A marriage is built through process.

One is **public**.

The other is **private**.

One takes **hours**.

The other takes **everything**.

We said we would love each other "for better or worse"—but no one really defines *worse* until it shows up.

And when it does, we start asking hard questions:

- *Did we mean what we said?*

- *Can I honor the vow when the feelings are gone?*

- *Was this covenant… or just ceremony?*

That's when faith enters — not faith in ourselves, but faith in the God who joined us in the first place.

When the Ring Is On but the Heart Is Closed

I have laid next to the woman I vowed to love…

…and felt galaxies apart.

Not from hatred — but from hurt.

We had the rings.

We had the house.

We had the last name.

But something essential was missing:

- **Intimacy.**

- **Tenderness.**

- **resence.**

- **Connection.**

The ceremony was real, yes — but if God didn't keep building, we would become covenant strangers sharing a bed.

That's the danger when the wedding becomes the goal, instead of the *starting line*.

God Wasn't Impressed by Our Ceremony — He Was Committed to Our Covenant

God does not attend weddings as a guest.

He attends as a **witness.**

He watches.

He seals.

He binds.

"What God has joined together..." (Matthew 19:6) is not about matching outfits or picture backgrounds.

It's about **divine agreement**.

Which means:

When things get hard — we don't run.

We return.

Not to the memory of the wedding day... but to the God who stood with us at the altar.

Because only He can teach us:

- How to love when it's painful,

- How to forgive when it's undeserved,

- How to grow when everything feels stuck.

After the Ceremony: Learning to Love Without an Audience

There is something sacred about loving someone when nobody else sees it.

- Washing dishes without applause.

- Praying over them while they sleep.

- Choosing silence instead of cutting words.

- Holding their hand when they don't know how badly they need touch.

That is where marriage lives.

Not in the aisle.

Not in the pictures.

But in the daily, quiet altar of choosing each other again — without music, without a microphone, without a crowd.

The Ceremony Is Over, But the Covenant Still Speaks

Here is the truth:

The ceremony may have ended… but the covenant still speaks.

It speaks in the quiet places.

It whispers in the dark moments.

It shouts when the enemy says, *"Walk away."*

It says:

"Stay.

Not because it's easy.

But because God is still in it."

He is still healing.

Still restoring.

Still strengthening.

Still building.

Even when the music stops.

Reflection Questions:

1. Have you ever felt like your marriage "ended" after the ceremony?

_____

_____

_____

_____

2. What moments in your relationship revealed the difference between performance and covenant?

_____

_____

_____

_____

3. In what ways have you allowed culture's view of marriage to shape your expectations?

_____

_____

_____

_____

4. How can you intentionally reengage in your relationship now that the "ceremony" is over?

_____

_____

_____

_____

Scripture Meditations:

- Psalm 127:1

- Ecclesiastes 4:9–12

- Matthew 19:6

- Malachi 2:14–16

- Ephesians 5:25–33

CONCLUSION

Love – The Unfinished Chapter What Should've Been Told

What *Should Have Been Told*

Love doesn't end at the altar.

It doesn't stop in the bedroom.

It doesn't die in disappointment.

Love — real, biblical love — is a journey of becoming.

Becoming more honest.

Becoming more healed.

Becoming more surrendered.

Becoming more like Christ.

The title of this book says it best:

Love is the unfinished chapter.

Because every day, God gives us a new page to write on.

And with His presence in the room… even the hardest chapters become holy.

So don't cry.

Don't give up.

Don't close the book.

Keep writing.

Keep loving.

Keep becoming.

Your story is not over — it's unfolding.

REFERENCES

1. **Holy Bible**, New International Version (NIV)

2. **Holy Bible**, New King James Version (NKJV)

3. *The Meaning of Marriage* — Timothy Keller

4. *Sacred Marriage* — Gary Thomas

5. *Love & Respect* — Dr. Emerson Eggerichs

6. "The Bible and Intimacy" — Desiring God Ministries

7. Marriage resource guides — Focus on the Family

8. Prayer & devotional notes by **Dr. Laron Matthews, PhD**

Booking Information

If you would like to invite **Dr. Laron Matthews** to speak at your church, conference, or event:

Phone: 877-912-2027

Website: www.werestoreu.org

Facebook: *Laron Matthews*

www.ingramcontent.com/pod-product-compliance
Lightning Source LLC
Chambersburg PA
CBHW060626100426
42744CB00008B/1515